Introduction

My mother sewed mostly from necessity, as our family was large and she needed to make every dollar count. She sewed items for the house and outfits for herself, my sister and me. They were not fancy, but I know they were most certainly sewn with love.

The first time I ever really paid attention to my mother's sewing was when I was 7 years old and a young lady from a neighboring farm asked Mom for help with a cowboy-style shirt. The fabric she was using was the prettiest shade of turquoise I had ever seen.

While the color of the shirt was certainly what drew me in, I was fascinated by the fact that someone was asking Mom for help with sewing. Didn't everyone's mother know how to sew?

As I grew older, Mom showed me the basics of her sewing machine, and I made a few dresses and shirts for myself as well as some doll clothes. In the process, I found my passion.

This book is for anyone and everyone who wants to learn the basics of sewing while creating fun projects through the combination of interesting fabric print and color combinations.

Each project in this book is designed to introduce a new technique while utilizing newly mastered skills from the previous project.

I hope you enjoy this book and make good use of your new skills, planning sewing projects and making them pretty with confidence.

Lorine

Meet the Designer

A passion for sewing and an eye for detail are the cornerstones of Lorine Mason's professional life.

An accomplished project designer, she is also the author of 12 crafting and sewing books, as well as the designer behind three pattern lines which are published under the name Lorine Mason Designs. She is also a licensed product designer.

Lorine currently writes the *Sewing Savvy* newsletter found at AnniesCatalog.com/Sewing_Savvy.php, as well as a personal blog available at www.lorinemason.com/blog.

She lives in Virginia with her husband, Bill.

2

Table of Contents

Dirndl Skirt Kitchen Towel, page 32

Smart Cookie Pot Holder, page 23

Eat-Dessert-First Place Mat, page 26

The Basics of Sewing

Interested in learning how to sew? Lucky you! You have come to exactly the right place to get started. After reviewing the basics and getting to know your machine, you will be ready to make a kitchen full of snappy accessories.

Getting to Know Your Sewing Machine

Whether you have a machine with manual controls or a top-of-the-line computerized machine, begin by reading through your sewing machine manual to become familiar with the basics of using your personal machine.

- Familiarize yourself with your machine's basic parts and all the attachments that are included with your machine. Learn how to connect your machine to a power supply and the foot control.

- Explore any built-in extras your machine may have, such as: a needle-down function that allows you to stop your machine with the needle in the down position each time, or an automatic thread cutter and backstitch at the end of a seam.

- Discover how to adjust stitch length and change needle position, and how to adjust and change presser feet on your machine.

- Learn and practice loading bobbins, inserting the bobbins into the machine, and threading your machine and needle.

- Explore all attachments that came with your machine. Your manual will give you instructions on how to add individual attachments to your machine and how to use those attachments.

Practice, Practice, Practice

Start your sewing experience by practicing the following: stitching straight stitch seams, pivoting to turn corners, stitching around curves and stitching samples of the stitches you have available on your machine.

Straight Stitching

- Thread your machine with a different color of thread in the bobbin and in the needle.

- Set your machine to stitch a medium-length straight stitch (about 10 stitches per inch).

- Align the edges of two layers of fabric right sides together and place them under the presser foot of your sewing machine.

- Position the fabric edges at the ¼-inch seam width marking on your sewing machine's stitch guide plate.

- Stitch 3 or 4 stitches. Use your reverse-stitch button to backstitch over the original stitches to lock the beginning of the seam.

- Continue stitching and carefully guide the fabric under the presser foot with the edge at the correct seam width marking. **Do not pull or push the fabric under the needle.** Your machine does it for you at an even speed.

Practice Tip

Using an old sewing machine needle, practice straight stitching on lined paper without thread before stitching on layers of fabric. Also, draw circles, curves, and inside and outside corners on paper to practice.

Paper dulls needles, so change your needle before attempting to sew on fabric.

Stitching Tip

Do not pull or push fabric through your sewing machine! *Pushing or pulling fabric will stretch the fabric and cause uneven stitches. You could also break needles and/or thread. Let the machine feed dogs do the work. Just carefully guide your fabric under the presser foot.*

- Stitch slowly to begin with, learning to control your fabric and machine, and then increase your speed. When you have completed a row of stitching, backstitch to secure the end of the seam. Trim the thread ends.

- Check your seam allowance. Is it a consistent ¼ inch wide? Practice until you are confident you can stitch the same width for the entire length of a seam. Try different widths: ⅜, ½ and ⅝ inch wide.

Stitching Tip

Position a strip of blue painter's tape along your stitch guide plate and over the machine bed to extend the stitching guidelines. You can also purchase a larger stitch guide to place over your machine's stitch guide plate.

Pivoting

To practice pivoting on corners:

- Use a ruler and fabric marker to draw right angles on wrong side of fabric (Figure 1).

Figure 1

- Stitch on a line to the point of the corner using a straight stitch. Stop stitching at the corner with the needle down in the fabric.

- Raise the presser foot and turn the fabric 90 degrees in the direction of the adjoining line. Lower the presser foot and continue stitching on the marked line.

- Lower the presser foot and continue stitching.

To practice pivoting around outside edges:

- Cut several 5-inch practice squares. Begin stitching along the side of one square with the fabric edge on the ¼-inch-wide stitch guide.

- Stitch to within ¼ inch of the next side at the first corner. Raise the presser foot and turn the fabric, positioning the next side along the ¼-inch-wide stitch guide, and continue stitching.

- Repeat for all four corners and sides. Continue practicing with 5-inch squares until you are comfortable with pivoting and can keep a consistent seam width.

Marking Tip

Mark the pivoting points on the wrong side of the fabric to make sure you pivot equidistantly from each side of the corner.

Stitching Curves

- Draw gentle curves on wrong side of one layer of fabric with a fabric marker (Figure 2).

Figure 2

- Position fabric under the presser foot and insert needle into fabric at the beginning of the curve.

- Stitch slowly so that you can guide the fabric while stitching on the curved line. It is sometimes helpful to shorten your stitch length when stitching curves.

- If the curves are tight, you may need to stitch a few stitches, raise the presser foot, pivot slightly, lower the presser foot and continue stitching.

Topstitching

A variation of straight stitching, topstitching is used to enhance a project using contrasting thread. It is done with topstitching thread, a specialty thread that is a heavier weight than general-purpose sewing thread. Use topstitching thread in the machine needle only; do not put it on the bobbin.

Edgestitching

Also a variation of straight stitching, edgestitching is used as a back-up seam to reinforce French seams, tabs or other details. Worked with general-purpose sewing thread, stitching is placed as close to the fabric edge as possible. Set the machine for short- to medium-length stitches.

Zigzag Stitching

A zigzag stitch looks exactly as it is described. It is a wide back-and-forth stitch that is used to cover more surface area than a straight stitch. This makes it perfect for securing the edges of loosely woven fabrics like monk's cloth. Adjust the length and the width settings for a stitch size that works best for you.

Decorative Stitches

Stitching a sampler of all the utility and decorative stitches available on your machine will help you understand how the machine makes these stitches. You will then be better able to integrate them into your projects.

• Draw straight lines on a solid-color fabric about 1½ inches apart with a fabric marker.

• Set your machine for a particular stitch referring to your manual for the correct setup. Thread machine with a different color in the needle and bobbin.

• Apply a different stitch along each marked line. Label each line with the stitch name and the machine setting.

The Essentials

There are several tools and supplies that every sewist (sewer + artist = sewist) needs in her sewing room or sewing box. There are beginner's tools that you can't do without and supplies that you will collect as you learn and then keep on hand for future projects.

Choosing Fabric

In today's fabric stores you will find much more than yards of fashion fabrics that are wound around large cardboard flats or tubes. There are many precut sizes available in 100 percent cotton for the quilter and sewist.

One of the most common precut sizes is the 18 x 22-inch rectangle called a fat quarter. Fat quarters are often sold in coordinating packs. Their bright colors and packaging attract sewists of all ages and are the perfect size for many projects—the exact reason that they have been chosen for many projects in this book.

This cut is the same amount of fabric in square inches as is a standard ¼-yard cut of 9 inches x 44/45 inches. Precut and yardage fabric requirements are listed in the materials lists in case you do not have precuts available to you.

Basic Sewing Supplies & Equipment

The "Basic sewing supplies and equipment" line in the materials list of each pattern contains what we suggest you have on hand when setting up a sewing area. Read through the material in The Essentials section of the general instructions for more information on some of these items.

• Sewing machine in good working order with zigzag stitch capability
• All-purpose thread to match fabric
• Hand-sewing needles and thimble
• Straight pins and pincushion
• Seam ripper
• Removable fabric-marking pens or tailor's chalk
• Measuring tools:
    tape measure
    variety clear sewing rulers
• Pattern tracing paper or cloth
• Point turner
• Pressing equipment:
    steam iron
    ironing board
    pressing cloths
• Scissors:
    fabric shears
    pinking shears
    paper scissors
• Seam sealant

Optional Supplies & Equipment
• Fabric spray adhesive
• Rotary cutter, mats and straightedges

Remember that the fabrics listed are suggestions only. We hope you will indulge your creative side and choose other prints and colors that delight you.

Preparing Fabric

Prewashing any washable fabric removes chemicals and excess dyes from the fabric and shrinks fabrics that are prone to shrinkage, such as 100 percent cotton. Prewash all fabrics the way you expect to wash the finished item, but do not use fabric softener. Add a color-catcher washing sheet to the washing cycle. Any dye that is released into the water will be absorbed by the washing sheet, rather than by the fabric.

Materials Tip

A little extra yardage has been added to the fabric amounts listed in the material lists to account for shrinkage, and to make it easier to straighten and still have enough fabric to cut out your project.

Prior to prewashing, you may want to finish all raw edges of any larger fabric pieces with a zigzag stitch. This prevents unraveling, especially if the fabric is a loose weave. If you do not finish the edges, trim all strings even with the raw edge. Press the pieces using a steam iron before cutting.

Battings, Stabilizers and Specialty Fabrics

Battings, interfacings and stabilizers provide structure and stability in sewing projects. They are chosen to match the fabric's characteristics, the construction techniques and the intended end use of the project. The types used in a project are listed in the materials list.

Heavy-weight fusible craft interfacing is a polyester blend that provides structure and support to projects.

100 percent cotton batting can be purchased in different lofts, or thicknesses, to match the project. You may want to use a thicker batting in a pot holder than that which you would use in a table runner or place mat. This type of batting is machine washable. Check to see if it has been preshrunk. It also comes as fusible or nonfusible.

Needlepunched insulating lining has a shiny side and a dull side. Use this batting in pot holders and casserole carriers. Apply the shiny side next to the heat source in order to reflect the heat away from hands.

Aluminized fabric, like that used for ironing board covers, is a 100 percent cotton fabric with an aluminized coating on one side. It is used in the same manner as the insulating lining to reflect heat away from hands.

Foam stabilizers are polyester foam with polyester fabric coverings. These stabilizers are used in items that require both stiffness and bulk.

Some of the projects also require specialty fabrics to meet the requirements of the intended use of the project. These are also listed in the project materials list.

Monk's cloth is a loose, even-weave 100 percent cotton fabric. Use a zigzag stitch to finish all cut edges of this fabric after cutting out a pattern and before construction to avoid unraveling.

Polyester netting is a soft, 100 percent polyester open-weave mesh.

Nonskid fabric is a lightweight canvas with raised nonskid dots or nonskid mesh on the back. This applied texture grips surfaces and prevents slipping.

Needles, Pins & Thread

Use a size 12 universal sewing machine needle for the projects in the book. Universal needles are good for general stitching and are available in sizes 60/8 to 120/19. Increase or decrease the size of your needle according to the weight of the fabric being stitched.

Pins can be purchased in different weights and lengths. For general sewing, purchase glass-head, nickel-plated, sharp or ballpoint pins approximately 1½ inches long.

Glass-head pins will not melt if the iron touches them. Ballpoint pins can be used for wovens and knits. The suggested length can be used to easily secure several layers of fabric and interfacing. Using pins with colored heads helps you see all the pins inserted in the fabric.

When pinning layers together, insert the pin perpendicular to the raw edges with the head hanging over for easy removal, or insert the pins in the seam line with the points toward the machine needle. Remove pins as you sew.

Stitching Tip

Never stitch over pins! If you happen to hit a pin with your machine needle you will damage the needle and pin, and quite possibly the sewing machine.

It's always wise to choose good-quality **thread**. A general-purpose–weight thread made of polyester, cotton, cotton blend or polyester-wrapped cotton works well with the fabrics suggested for the projects in this book.

Purchase threads that match the project fabrics. If using a multicolored fabric, choose a thread that will blend with the predominant color. If desired, choose a contrasting color for topstitching. Topstitching thread is heavier so it will sit on top of the fabric, making it an eye-catching design element in the project.

Ironing Tools

To construct a quality finished project you will need to iron and press correctly. Choose an iron that has steam- and dry-ironing capabilities and switches itself off after a certain amount of time. You will find it easier to do your ironing/pressing on a standard ironing board that can be adjusted to your height.

Set your iron on an appropriate heat setting for the fabric referring to your iron's manual. The cotton steam setting can be used for all the fabrics suggested in this book.

It is a good idea to purchase an iron sole plate that protects the sole of your iron from damage and residue from iron-on products. Use a pressing cloth when ironing/pressing specialty fabrics.

Technique Tip

Remember that there is a difference between ironing and pressing. Ironing is moving the iron across the fabric without raising the iron or applying pressure. Be careful because you can stretch the fabric. Do this to remove wrinkles for cutting preparation.

Pressing is done by lowering the iron onto the fabric, applying moderate pressure and steam, and then raising the iron straight up off the surface before moving it to another area. This will eliminate stretching and allow steam to permeate the fabric giving you crisp seam lines, sharp corners and flat edges.

Embellishments

The embellishments that are used in this book can be purchased at your local fabric store and are made by different manufacturers.

Piping is used to define a seam and add interest. It is a bias strip of fabric folded over cotton cord and stitched to secure. You can purchase piping by the yard or in packages in a variety of widths and colors, or you can make your own.

Technique Tip

To make your own piping, cut bias strips at least twice the diameter of the piping cord plus twice the seam allowance. If using ¼-inch cord cut bias strips 1 inch wide for a ¼-inch seam allowance or 1½ inches wide for a ½-inch seam allowance.

Stitch the strips together with a ¼-inch angled seam; press seams to one side. Wrap the cord with the bias strip, matching the long edges and pinning close to the cord.

Using a zipper foot, stitch as close as possible to the cord, making sure the bias strip is wrapped tightly.

Rickrack is a flat trim woven in a zigzag pattern. It is generally used as a surface trim, but it can be inserted into a seam to give a scalloped-edge appearance. It is sold by the yard or in packages in a variety of widths and colors.

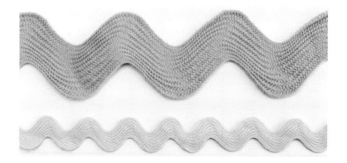

Grosgrain ribbon has a ribbed center and bound edges. If using this on a washable project make sure to purchase a washable ribbon for garments. It is sold in a wide variety of widths and colors by the yard, spool or package.

Cutting Tools & Techniques

Quality cutting tools are an essential part of sewing. As a general rule, purchase the best-quality cutting tools you can afford and take good care of them. Keep them sharp and they will cut easily and accurately. There is nothing more aggravating than trying to cut through fabric with dull shears or a dull rotary cutter.

Shears & Scissors

There is a difference between shears and scissors; however, note that the term "scissors" is commonly used for both items.

Shears have blades longer than 6 inches with different handle loops for your thumb and fingers.

Scissors have blades less than 6 inches in length with identical handle loops.

When cutting, the blades of shears/scissors should slide through the fabric smoothly with each cut. Generally, a sewist will use the larger shears to cut patterns from the fabric and will reserve the smaller scissors to clip curves and trim threads.

Cutting Tip

Paper and other non-fabric materials dull cutting edges quickly. Have separate tools for your sewing room. Never use your sewing shears, scissors or rotary cutters to cut anything other than fabric.

Seam Rippers

A seam or stitch ripper is specifically designed for unpicking or ripping out seams and errant stitches. Seam rippers should be used carefully so as not to damage the fabric. There are pointed, bladed and scissor styles. Use the style that gives you the most control.

When using the pointed style, insert the tip under the top or bottom thread of the seam. Cut through the thread only. Don't pierce the fabric with the tip.

Rotary Cutter, Mat & Ruler

If your budget allows, purchase these time-saving tools and master the art of using a rotary cutter, self-healing mat and clear plastic ruler. Because you hold the fabric in place with the ruler, and keep the blade on the cutting surface, the fabric is less likely to move and you are able to achieve a clean and straight cut. Be aware that you will still need scissors on hand to cut curves and to trim threads.

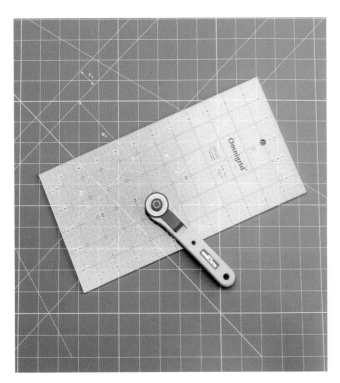

As a beginner, purchase an 18 x 24-inch cutting board, a 6 x 18-inch clear rotary-cutting ruler and a 28mm rotary cutter.

Cutting Tip

Rotary-cutter blades are especially sharp.

You can cut up to six layers of fabric at the

same time. Never leave the blade uncovered!

Always close the blade cover when you lay

the cutter on the work surface.

Cutting With a Rotary Cutter

Carefully straighten your fat quarters or fabric yardage before cutting. Press your fabric to remove wrinkles and fold lines. Fold selvages together, making sure the fabric hangs straight (Figure 3). ***Note:** Drawings show fat quarters.*

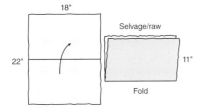

Figure 3

Align the selvage edges on a grid of the cutting mat; trim one of the raw edges perpendicular to the selvage, cutting away the minimum amount of fabric needed to cut an even edge (Figure 4). Position this edge on a grid and straighten another edge; repeat to straighten remaining raw edge sides.

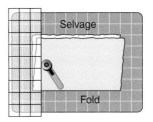

Figure 4

When you are rotary-cutting, first cut a strip the required width across the fabric and then cut squares, rectangles and triangles as instructed. (Figure 5).

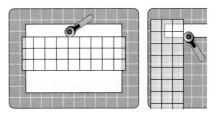

Figure 5

Always measure twice and cut once!

Using Patterns

A pattern is provided for a fabric piece that is a unique shape. Photocopy or trace the shape and cut along the marked edge. Pin the pattern piece on the fabric and cut along the paper edge.

Sewing Techniques

You will be using several machine- and hand-stitching techniques throughout this book. You will find the technique(s) used in each project listed after the cutting instructions. Please refer to this section for details of these techniques. You may also want to have a complete sewing guide in your sewing room. Check out some at your local library to find one that works for you before purchasing one.

At the beginning of all assembly instructions you will see the seam allowance that you should use during construction. For most of the projects in this book, you will stitch a ½-inch seam allowance.

Standard Seam
Refer to Straight Stitching on page 3 in the Practice, Practice, Practice section to stitch a standard seam with fabric pieces right sides together. Use a coordinating-color thread in the needle and bobbin of your sewing machine.

Backstitch at the beginning and end of each seam to keep it from coming apart during construction.

French Seam
Pin fabric pieces wrong sides together and stitch a ¼-inch seam (Figure 6a). Press seam flat. Trim seam allowance to ⅛ inch (Figure 6b).

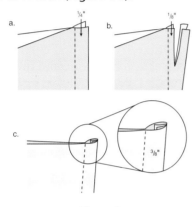

Figure 6

Turn fabric pieces right sides together and press seam flat. Pin and stitch again using a ⅜-inch seam allowance to encase the previous seam allowance, referring to Figure 6c. Press seam to one side.

Double-Turned Hems
Apply a basting tape to the right side of the fabric along the hem raw edge following the manufacturer's instructions. Fold fabric ¼ inch to wrong side and press (Figure 7a). *Note: You can use either a ¼-inch-wide fusible tape or a sticky basting tape. Both have paper backings. The fusible tape requires you to heat-set it. The sticky tape can be finger-pressed in place. If using the sticky tape, do not apply until after folds have been pressed in place.*

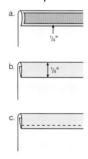

Figure 7

Fold again to wrong side by the amount indicated in instructions and press (Figure 7b). Remove paper backing on basting tape. If using fusible tape, re-press hem. *Note: Drawings show ¼-inch double-turned hem.*

Edgestitch along the first folded edge as shown in Figure 7c.

Making Bias or Straight-Grain Seam Binding
Binding can be purchased in a variety of solid colors and widths cut on the bias, or you can make your own straight-grain or bias binding in the fabric and size you need.

Bias binding should be used on curved seams and edges because it conforms to the curve without puckering. You can also use bias binding on straight seams and straight edges. Straight-grain binding should be used on straight seams and straight edges only.

Making Straight-Grain Binding
Cut 2-inch-wide strips x the fabric width (if using fat quarters use the 22-inch edge as the fabric width).

Referring to Figure 8, join strips together with diagonal seams and trim seam allowances to ¼ inch. Press seams open. Fold strip in half wrong sides together along length and press.

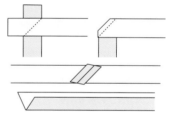

Figure 8

To distribute the bulk of the fabric layers evenly, cut one short end at a 45-degree angle and press ½ inch to wrong side on one short end and re-press binding strip in half lengthwise (Figure 9).

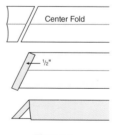

Figure 9

Making Bias Binding

Cut a large square of fabric in half diagonally to make two triangles (Figure 10). *Note: An 18-inch square will make 162 inches of 2-inch-wide bias binding.*

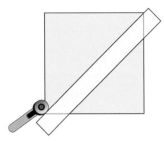

Figure 10

Referring to Figure 11, align and stitch two short triangle edges right sides together using a ¼-inch seam. Press seam open.

Figure 11

With wrong side up, mark cutting lines parallel to the bias edges referring to Figure 12.

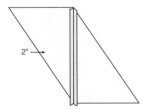

Figure 12

Form a tube by bringing the right sides of the fabric together and offsetting the ends so that the cutting lines match (Figure 13). Stitch a ¼-inch seam; press open. Cut along cutting lines to make one long bias strip.

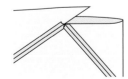

Figure 13

Cut one short end at a 45-degree angle, press ½ inch to wrong side on one short end and re-press binding strip in half lengthwise referring again to Figure 9.

Applying Seam Binding

Two methods of applying seam binding are used in this book. Project instructions will refer to these methods.

If you are using a purchased binding for both of these methods, prepare the binding for use by opening it flat. Trim one short end of the binding strip at a 45-degree angle and turn to wrong side ½ inch; press. Re-press binding in half lengthwise with wrong sides together.

Method 1

Position folded short end of binding to right side of project matching raw edges. Pin and stitch binding around project.

To make mitered corners for square corners, begin stitching approximately 4 inches from end and stitch around project using a ¼-inch seam. Stop stitching ¼ inch from corner and backstitch (Figure 14).

Figure 14

Remove from machine and fold binding up at a 45-degree angle to seam and then down even with project edges, forming a pleat at corner, referring to Figure 15.

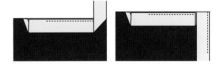

Figure 15

Resume stitching from corner edge as shown in Figure 15 and stitch down project side, stopping ¼ inch from next corner. Repeat, mitering all corners and stitching to within 4 inches of starting point.

Trim binding end long enough to tuck inside starting end and complete stitching (Figure 16).

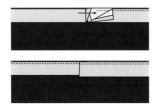

Figure 16

Turn binding to wrong side of project over seam and hand-stitch binding in place using a slip stitch, referring to Slip Stitch on page 13.

Method 2

Fold long raw edges of binding strip to center fold and press. Re-press center fold to make a double-fold binding.

Position and pin folded short end of binding over edge or seam to be bound, encasing all layers in binding (Figure 17).

Figure 17

Pin around project. Trim and tuck end under beginning end by 1 inch (Figure 18).

Figure 18

Edgestitch through all layers, catching both binding edges referring to Figure 19.

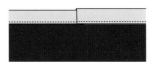

Figure 19

Technique Tip

Binding Method 2 can be accomplished more easily by basting the binding in place before topstitching, making sure you are catching both sides of the binding in the stitching.

Alternatively, unfold the binding and match one raw binding edge to the wrong side of the edge being bound. Pin in place to secure. Stitch along the first fold line. Wrap the binding over to the right side matching the folded edge to the seam and pin. Topstitch along this binding edge. You will easily catch both sides of the binding in the stitching.

Hand Sewing

It is necessary to stitch some things by hand. For general-purpose hand sewing, you should purchase a variety pack of nickel-plated sharp needles. Larger-number needle sizes indicate finer needles. Select a needle size for the fabric weight you are stitching. For example, use a size 8 needle for medium-weight fabric like 100 percent cotton.

Use the same general-purpose thread you are using in your sewing machine. Thread the needle and knot one end. Sew with a single strand of thread unless otherwise instructed.

Basting

Basting holds layers, binding and trim in place when pins aren't practical or sufficient, and it does not have to be removed prior to final stitching. It is also much more secure than pinning.

Materials Tip

Purchase basting tape or paper-backed fusible tape like Steam-A-Seam 2® tape instead of pins or thread for basting.

Apply to seam allowances, hems and binding to hold secure while doing final stitching.

Follow manufacturer's instructions to apply.

Referring to Figure 20, bring a contrasting-color knotted thread through the layers from back to front and take long stitches that will hold but can be removed easily.

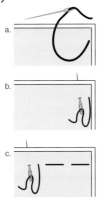

Figure 20

Basting can also be done on your sewing machine by using the maximum stitch length.

Ladder Stitch

A ladder stitch is a nearly invisible way to join the folded edges of two fabrics from the right side. This stitch may be used in situations where an opening has been left for turning a piece right side out (like a pillow cover).

Figure 21

Bring a knotted thread up from the wrong side at the seam fold. Take a stitch into the opposite side picking up only 2 or 3 threads of the fabric. Continue stitching from side to side, gently pulling the thread to close the seam.

Slip Stitch

The slip stitch is a hemming stitch that is also used to apply bindings when you do not want stitching to be visible.

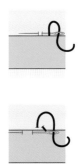

Slip Stitch

Bring the needle up through the hem fold burying the knot of your thread in the hem fold. Slide the needle into the hem's folded edge and inside the fold, coming out about ¼ inch away. Take a stitch of about 2 or 3 fabric threads just above the hem fold and go back into the fold as before.

Sewing Buttons

Using double thread, knot the ends and bring needle up from wrong side of fabric at button placement and through a buttonhole. With button held against the fabric, insert needle through a second buttonhole and fabric to wrong side.

Repeat coming up through first hole and down through second several times. Knot thread on wrong side and trim thread tail close to fabric.

For buttons with four holes, stitch through holes in an "X" pattern. ∎

Can-Do Dishcloth

One side works while the other side cheers! By backing merry prints with hardworking textures, all kitchen tasks are made brighter, from picking up spills to polishing glass.

Finished Size
11 x 11 inches

Materials
- 1 fat quarter or ⅜ yard cotton print
- ⅜ yard monk's cloth
- Coordinating thread
- Basic sewing supplies and equipment

Fabric Choices

Substitute any of these utility fabrics for monk's cloth:

- Waffle weave
- Huck toweling
- Terry cloth*
- Diaper cloth

*Terry cloth comes in a wide variety of colors that can be coordinated with your print.

Cutting

From cotton print:
- Cut 1 (12-inch) square.

From monk's cloth:
- Cut 1 (12-inch) square.

Sewing Techniques*
Machine stitching:
  Straight stitching
  Topstitching
  Zigzag stitching
*Refer to The Basics of Sewing on page 3.

Assembly
Use a ½-inch seam allowance and stitch right sides together unless otherwise indicated.

1. Finish all edges of the monk's cloth square with a zigzag stitch to prevent edges from fraying during construction.

2. Layer and pin print and monk's cloth squares right sides together, matching outside edges.

3. Stitch around the outside edges, pivoting at corners. Leave a 3-inch opening along one side for turning (Figure 1).

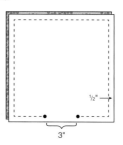

Figure 1

4. Clip corners at an angle referring to Figure 2.

Figure 2

5. Turn dishcloth right side out through opening. Turn opening seam allowances to inside and pin in place. Press edges flat.

6. Topstitch around dishcloth ¼ inch from edge and again ¼ inch from first stitching to complete the dishcloth (Figure 3). ∎

Figure 3

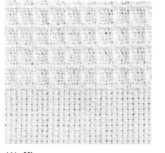

Waffle weave.

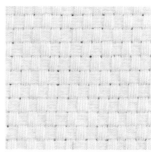

Monk's cloth.

Blue Ribbon Tea Towel

If a kitchen towel is for work, and a tea towel is for display,
this easy-to-make beauty will certainly steal the show.

Finished Size
20 x 26 inches

Materials
- 1 fat quarter or ⅛ yard orange tonal
- 1 fat quarter or ¼ yard each orange floral and yellow print
- 1 fat quarter or ½ yard yellow floral
- Coordinating thread
- Basic sewing supplies and equipment

Cutting

From orange tonal:
- Cut 1 (3 x 22-inch) rectangle.

From orange floral:
- Cut 1 (6 x 22-inch) rectangle.

From yellow print:
- Cut 1 (6 x 22-inch) rectangle.

From yellow floral:
- Cut 1 (16 x 22-inch) rectangle.

Stitch Technique Tip

To begin a seam that is thick, like the corners of the towel's top and bottom hems, lengthen the stitches. Raise the presser foot, position the beginning of the seam under the needle and then lower the needle into the fabric.

Fold a scrap of fabric the same thickness as the seam and place the folded scrap behind the seam beginning. Lower the presser foot and begin stitching, holding the thread tails.

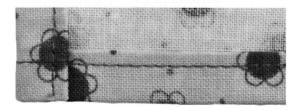

Sewing Techniques*
Machine stitching:
  Straight stitching
  Topstitching
  French seam
  Double-turned hem
Refer to The Basics of Sewing on page 3.

Assembly
Use a ½-inch seam allowance and stitch right sides together unless otherwise indicated. Note that the first step of a French seam uses a ¼" seam allowance.

1. Referring to Figure 1 for order, stitch the orange and yellow floral rectangles together using a French seam.

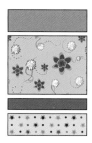

Figure 1   **Figure 2**

2. Press the seam toward the yellow floral rectangle and topstitch ¼ inch from the seam through all layers (Figure 2).

3. Repeat to stitch and topstitch all rectangles together pressing seam allowances, referring to arrows in Figure 3.

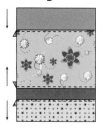

Figure 3   **Figure 4**

4. Stitch a ½-inch double-turned hem on both long sides of the towel and then on the top and bottom (Figure 4). ■

General Tip

The French seams and double-turned hems ensure that these charming towels will withstand washing after washing.

Sitting Pretty Shelf & Drawer Liners

Illuminate every nook and cranny in your kitchen with colorful cotton liners. The perfect pairing of pretty (flowered fabric) and practical (nonskid backing), they will stay in place while protecting work and storage surfaces.

Finished Size
Shelf or drawer measurements

Determining Shelf/Drawer Size & Yardage
Measure the interior width and depth of either the shelf or drawer referring to Figure 1.

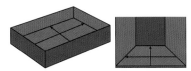

Figure 1

Add 1 inch to each measurement to determine the size rectangle or square needed to make the liner. Purchase enough fabric and nonskid backing yardage to cut the determined size.

For example, if the drawer's inside measurements are 15 inches wide x 22 inches long, you will cut 16 x 23-inch rectangles. This means you will need to purchase ½ yard each of fabric and nonskid backing.

Materials
- Yardage determined for cotton print and nonskid backing referring to Determining Shelf/Drawer Size & Yardage
- Coordinating thread
- Basic sewing supplies and equipment

Cutting
- Cut 1 rectangle the determined size from the cotton print and nonskid backing referring to Determining Shelf/Drawer Size & Yardage.

Sewing Techniques*
Machine stitching:
  Straight stitching
  Topstitching
Hand stitching:
  Slip stitch
Refer to The Basics of Sewing on page 3.

Nonskid backing fabric.

Assembly

Use a ½-inch seam allowance and stitch right sides together unless otherwise indicated.

1. Layer and pin print and nonskid backing rectangles right sides together matching outside edges.

2. Stitch around outside edges pivoting at corners. Leave a 3-inch opening along one side for turning (Figure 2).

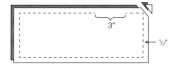

Figure 2

3. Clip corners at an angle referring again to Figure 2.

4. Turn liner right side out through opening. Turn opening seam allowances to inside and pin in place. Press edges flat.

5. Topstitch around liner ¼ inch from edge to complete the liner (Figure 3). ■

Figure 3

Laundering Tip

Don't worry about unavoidable drips and spills because all the materials for these liners are machine washable.

Short & Sweet Apron

This apron is small on coverage but big on pockets. Add three decorative buttons to the ribbon waistband and move from island, to oven to fridge in style.

Finished Size
15 x 21 inches (not including ties)

Materials
- ⅓ yard orange print
- ⅝ yard green floral
- 2½ yards 1-inch-wide coordinating grosgrain ribbon
- 3 (⅝-inch-diameter) coordinating buttons
- Coordinating thread
- ¼-inch-wide basting tape
- Basic sewing supplies and equipment

Cutting

From orange print:
- Cut 1 (10½ x 22-inch) rectangle for pocket.

From green floral:
- Cut 1 (18 x 22-inch) rectangle for apron.

Sewing Techniques*
Machine stitching:
 Straight stitching
 Topstitching
 Edgestitching
 Double-turned hems
Refer to The Basics of Sewing on page 3.

Assembly
Use a ½-inch seam allowance and stitch right sides together unless otherwise indicated.

1. Apply basting tape to wrong side of one 22-inch-wide end of pocket. Fold edge ¼ inch to wrong side (Figure 1).

Figure 1

2. Turn and press folded edge 1¼ inch to wrong side and edgestitch along first fold (Figure 2).

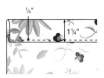

Figure 2

3. Layer and pin pocket right side down on wrong side of apron rectangle matching raw 22-inch bottom edges; stitch together (Figure 3a).

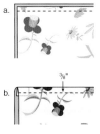

Figure 3

4. Press pocket to right side of apron and topstitch ⅜ inch from seam (Figure 3b).

5. Draw two lines 7 inches from each side of the apron to divide pocket (Figure 4). Stitch through all layers on the marked lines, backstitching both ends of stitching to secure.

Figure 4

6. Stitch a ½-inch double-turned hem in the apron sides treating the apron and pocket as a single layer.

7. To make a casing for the ribbon ties, refer to steps 1 and 2, stitching the casing into the top raw edge of the apron.

Pocket Corners Tip

To add more strength to a pocket corner, take a tip from men's ready-wear garments.

At the top of a pocket seam (either an outside pocket corner or a dividing seam as in the apron), stitch to the top of the pocket and then stitch a narrow triangle at the top.
It doesn't have to be large to keep the pocket from pulling away from the body of the garment when used.

8. Attach a safety pin to one end of the grosgrain ribbon and feed that end through the casing. Center the ribbon in the casing and pin along sides of apron to hold.

9. Find the center of the apron casing and sew one button to center, sewing through all layers; measure 1 inch on either side of the center button to mark placement for buttons (Figure 5). Stitch remaining buttons through all layers.

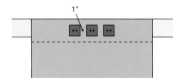

Figure 5

10. Trim ribbon ends at an angle to help prevent fraying. ■

Smart Cookie Pot Holder

Everyone knows that cookies are made of butter and love.
This clever pot holder is made of batting and aluminized fabric.
Make a dozen because you can never have enough of a good thing.

Finished Size
8 x 8 inches

Materials
- 1 fat quarter or ¼ yard floral print
- 1 fat quarter or ¼ yard print
- ¼ yard aluminized fabric
- ⅜ yard or craft size packaged cotton batting
- Coordinating thread
- Basic sewing supplies and equipment

Cutting
From floral print:
- Cut 1 (2 x 7-inch) strip for hanging loop.
- Cut 1 (9-inch) square.
    Subcut on 1 diagonal to make 2 triangles.

From print:
- Cut 2 (9-inch) squares.
    Subcut 1 square on 1 diagonal to make
    2 triangles.

From aluminized fabric:
- Cut 1 (9-inch) square.

From cotton batting:
- Cut 3 (9-inch) squares.
    Subcut 1 square on 1 diagonal to
    make 2 triangles.

Sewing Techniques*
Machine stitching:
    Straight stitching
    Topstitching
    Edgestitching
Hand stitching:
    Basting stitch (optional)
    Slip stitch
*Refer to The Basics of Sewing on page 3.

Assembly
Use a ½-inch seam allowance and stitch right
sides together unless otherwise indicated.

1. Fold and press the 2 x 7-inch floral print strip
in half wrong sides together. Unfold and fold and
press in long sides ½ inch to wrong side. Re-press
along center fold (Figure 1a).

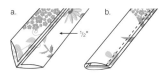

Figure 1

2. Edgestitch along double-folded edge, stitching
through all layers referring to Figure 1b. Set aside
for hanging loop.

3. Layer one of each fabric triangle, right sides together, with a batting triangle on top; pin together and stitch along the long edge of the triangles (Figure 2). Repeat with remaining triangles.

Figure 2

4. Trim batting close to seam and turn triangles right side out with batting between; press edge flat. Topstitch ¼ inch from long side, referring again to Figure 2.

5. Layer together the two squares of cotton batting; remaining print square, right side up; and the assembled triangles with floral print side up, referring to Figure 3, and pin or baste in place. *Note: Match triangle raw edges to square raw edges. There will be space between triangle topstitched edges.*

Figure 3

6. Fold the hanging loop strip from step 2 in half and pin in top left corner of pot holder with folded end toward center of pot holder (Figure 4).

Figure 4

7. Position aluminized fabric square, aluminized side down, on the layered pot holder (Figure 5). Pin all layers together and baste by hand or machine.

Figure 5

8. Stitch around pot holder outer edges leaving a 4-inch opening on one side (Figure 6).

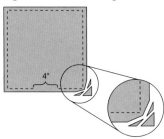

Figure 6

9. Clip batting close to seam and corners at an angle to reduce bulk referring again to Figure 6.

10. Turn pot holder right side out, carefully pushing out corners. Turn opening seam allowance to inside and press all edges flat.

11. Hand-stitch opening closed using a slip stitch. ■

Eat-Dessert-First Place Mat

Along with protecting your tabletop, a place mat acts as a nice soft frame that accentuates your place setting and your food. A winning place mat will make your ice cream creamier and your chocolate sauce saucier, so dig in!

Finished Sizes
Place Mat: 15 x 18 inches
Napkin: 17 x 17 inches

Materials
Note: *Materials listed are for 1 each place mat and napkin.*

- 1 fat quarter of each or yardage listed:
  - ⅛ yard red print
  - ¼ yard mint berry
  - ⅓ yard orange floral
  - ½ yard green print
  - ½ yard mint print
- ½ yard cotton batting
- Coordinating thread
- 1 (½-inch-diameter) flat button
- ¼-inch-wide basting tape
- Basic sewing supplies and equipment

Cutting

From red print:
- Cut 1 (9 x 4-inch) rectangle for pocket.

From mint berry:
- Cut 2 (2½ x 12-inch) side border strips.
- Cut 2 (2½ x 19-inch) top/bottom border strips.

From orange floral:
- Cut 1 (12 x 16-inch) rectangle for place mat center panel.

From green print:
- Cut 1 (18 x 18-inch) rectangle for napkin.

From mint print:
- Cut 1 (16 x 19-inch) backing rectangle.

From cotton batting:
- Cut 1 (16 x 19-inch) rectangle.

Sewing Techniques*
Machine stitching:
  Straight stitching
  Topstitching
  Edgestitching
Hand stitching:
  Slip stitch
Refer to The Basics of Sewing on page 3.

Place Mat Assembly
Use a ½-inch seam allowance and stitch right sides together unless otherwise indicated.

1. Fold pocket rectangle in half to make a 4 x 4½–inch rectangle. Stitch 4½-inch raw edges together on one side (Figure 1). Turn right side out and press edges flat.

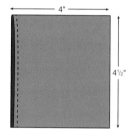

Figure 1

2. Position pocket with seamed edge to the left and folded edge at top. Fold down top left corner and stitch button to flap to secure (Figure 2).

Figure 2

Figure 3

3. Position and pin pocket in right bottom corner of place mat center panel matching raw edges and edgestitch seamed edge of pocket from folded corner to bottom (Figure 3).

4. Stitch side border strips to opposite sides of place mat center panel catching pocket in right-hand side seam (Figure 4). Press seams toward borders.

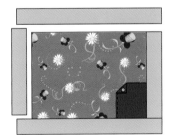

Figure 4

5. Stitch top/bottom border strips to place mat center panel referring again to Figure 4. Press seams toward borders.

6. Layer and pin together cotton batting; place mat top, right side up; and backing, wrong side up (Figure 5).

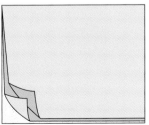

Figure 5

7. Stitch around outside edges leaving a 4-inch opening on one long side. Trim batting close to seam and clip corners at an angle to reduce bulk (Figure 6).

Figure 6

8. Turn place mat right side out through opening, gently pushing corners out. Push opening seam allowances to inside and press edges flat. Hand-stitch opening closed using a slip stitch.

Slip Stitch

9. Topstitch ½ inch from outside edge of place mat. Straight stitch in the seam between borders and place mat center referring to red stitching lines in Figure 7.

Figure 7

Napkin Assembly

Use a ½-inch seam allowance and stitch right sides together unless otherwise indicated.

1. Apply basting tape to a right-side edge of the napkin square (Figure 8a) referring to manufacturer's instructions.

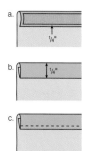

Figure 8

2. Fold fabric ¼ inch to wrong side (the width of the basting tape). Fold ¼ inch to wrong side again making a ¼-inch double-turned hem and press (Figure 8b).

3. Edgestitch along first fold referring to Figure 8c to complete hem on one side of napkin.

4. Repeat steps 1–3 to hem opposite side of napkin and then remaining sides to complete napkin (Figure 9). ◼

Figure 9

General Tip

To catch drips or crumbs, a wink of a pocket keeps a nice soft napkin handy. Instructions are included for a 17-inch-square napkin, but you can make yours larger or smaller for the size that works best for you.

Runway Table Runner

To create a chic tablescape, begin with a high-fashion table runner. A beautiful runner is always in season, acting as a must-have layer that beautifies any table and highlights any centerpiece.

Finished Size
15 x 41 inches

Materials
- 1 fat quarter or ¼ yard each olive berry and red print
- ½ yard each green solid and green floral
- ½ yard cotton batting
- 2 yards coordinating purchased piping
- 9 (½-inch-diameter) flat buttons (optional)
- Coordinating thread
- Zipper foot
- Basic sewing supplies and equipment

Materials Tips

Sample uses purchased red piping and nine yellow buttons. You may want to change the color of piping and buttons, and adjust the number of buttons to enhance the print you have purchased for the center of your table runner.

Cutting

From olive berry:
- Cut 2 (5 x 16-inch) rectangles for inner borders.

From red print:
- Cut 2 (7 x 16-inch) rectangles for outer borders.

From green solid:
- Cut 1 (16 x 42-inch) rectangle for backing.

From green floral:
- Cut 1 (16 x 22-inch) rectangle for center panel.

From cotton batting:
- Cut 1 (16 x 42-inch) rectangle.

From purchased piping:
- Cut 4 (16-inch) lengths.

Sewing Techniques*
Machine stitching:
  Straight stitching
  Topstitching
Hand stitching:
  Slip stitch
Refer to The Basics of Sewing on page 3.

Assembly

Use a ½-inch seam allowance and stitch right sides together unless otherwise indicated.

1. Attach zipper foot to your sewing machine referring to your manual. Set needle position on left side of foot.

2. Position and pin piping to short sides of center panel. Stitch close to the piping referring to Figure 1.

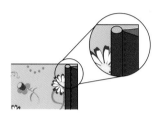

Figure 1

3. Stitch the inner border rectangles to the center panel matching 16-inch ends and stitching close to piping again (Figure 2). Press seams toward the center panel.

Figure 2

4. Repeat steps 2 and 3 adding piping and outer borders to inner borders.

5. Layer and pin together cotton batting; assembled top, right side up; and backing, wrong side up (Figure 3).

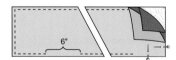

Figure 3

6. Stitch around outside edges leaving a 6-inch opening on one long edge referring again to Figure 3.

7. Clip batting close to seam allowance and corners at an angle to reduce bulk (Figure 4).

Figure 4

8. Turn table runner right side out. Turn edges of opening to inside and press edges flat.

9. Hand-stitch opening closed using a slip stitch.

10. Topstitch ½ inch away from all outside edges.

11. Embellish and quilt as desired. ▪

Securing Batting Tip

The sample has buttons stitched through all layers in the table runner center section at large flower centers. This helps hold the batting in place during laundering.

You can also do an allover meandering quilting pattern in the quilt center and borders (Figure A).

Figure A

General Tip
Consider using this pattern
to make runners for a buffet,
credenza or coffee table.

Dirndl Skirt Kitchen Towel

The gathered skirts and rickrack trim of this flouncy kitchen towel will make you want to dance. Made from thirsty layers of textured cotton, this cook's companion works hard, plays hard and then works again. Cue the polka music!

Finished Size
11 x 19 inches

Materials
- 1 fat quarter or ¼ yard each red floral and orange print
- ½ yard monk's cloth
- Coordinating thread
- 2 (4-inch) pieces hook-and-loop sticky-back tape
- ¼-inch-wide basting tape
- 1 package each coordinating ½-inch-wide and 1½-inch-wide rickrack
- 2 flat buttons each 1 inch and ½ inch in diameter
- Basic sewing supplies and equipment

Fabric Choices

Substitute any of these utility fabrics for monk's cloth:
- *Waffle weave*
- *Huck toweling*
- *Terry cloth**
- *Diaper cloth*

*Terry cloth comes in a wide variety of colors that can be coordinated with your print.

Cutting

From red floral:
- Cut 1 each Top Tab and Bottom Tab using patterns provided on pages 35 and 36. Transfer all markings to fabric.

From orange print:
- For lining, cut 1 each Top Tab and Bottom Tab using patterns provided on pages 35 and 36. Transfer all markings to fabric.

From monk's cloth:
- Cut 1 (16 x 20-inch) rectangle for towel bottom layer.
- Cut 1 (12 x 20-inch) rectangle for towel top layer.
- **Note:** *Because monk's cloth is a very loose weave, finish all raw edges with zigzag stitches to prevent fraying during construction.*

Sewing Techniques*
Machine stitching:
  Straight stitching
  Topstitching
  Gathering
  Edgestitching
  Zigzag stitching
  Double-turned hem
Hand stitching:
  Slip stitch
*Refer to The Basics of Sewing on page 3.

Assembly

Use a ½-inch seam allowance and stitch right sides together unless otherwise indicated.

1. Apply hook-and-loop tape pieces to Top Tab lining where marked. Topstitch around all four sides of both hook-and-loop tape pieces to secure.

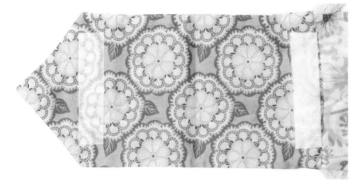

2. Stitch Top Tab and Top Tab lining together leaving the straight edge open. Repeat with the Bottom Tab and Bottom Tab lining (Figure 1). Trim corners at an angle to reduce bulk (Figure 2).

½"

Figure 1   **Figure 2**

3. Turn tabs right side out, gently pushing out corners, and press edges flat. Turn the open ends of the tabs to inside ½ inch and press flat.

4. Center large button on right side of Top Tab at marked point. Place small button on top of large button and stitch through both buttons and Top Tab to secure.

Time-Saver Tip

Eliminate cutting and hemming fabric for the towel by substituting a plain white cotton tea towel. Use the width of the tea towel and simply cut two lengths: 14½ inches and 11½ inches.

5. Stitch ¼-inch double-turned hems in one long side and both short ends of both monk's cloth rectangles referring to Sewing Techniques, Double-Turned Hems on page 10 in The Basics of Sewing.

6. Position and pin ½-inch rickrack on towel top layer, just above the 20-inch side hem stitching. Stitch through the middle of the rickrack to secure (Figure 3a). ***Note:*** *Instead of using pins, apply basting tape to wrong side of rickrack and then position on towel edge.*

a.   b.

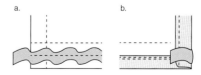

Figure 3

7. Turn ends of rickrack to wrong side and hand-stitch to towel hems using a slip stitch (Figure 3b).

8. Position and pin 1½-inch-wide rickrack on towel bottom layer, centering it over the 20-inch side hem stitching. ***Note:*** *The rickrack will show below the hemmed edge.*

9. Edgestitch along the top edge of the rickrack (Figure 4). Turn ends of rickrack to wrong side and hand-stitch to towel hems using a slip stitch, referring to Figure 3b.

Figure 4

10. Pin-mark 2 inches in from each side and gather the remaining long edge of one towel rectangle between the pins to approximately 10½ inches referring to Gathering Edges on page 35. Repeat for the second rectangle.

11. Layer and pin together top and bottom layers with right sides up and matching raw edges. Fold towel sides inward to wrong side until top raw edge measure 4⅜ inches wide (Figure 5). Hand- or machine-baste all layers together.

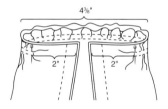

Figure 5

General Tip

This Dirndl Skirt Kitchen Towel can easily move around the room with you. Attach and reattach to knobs or handles with the help of sturdy hook-and-loop strips.

12. Layer Bottom Tab orange print side against towel top layer side matching raw edges, and stitch (Figure 6).

Figure 6

Stitch Technique Tip

To stitch a seam that is thick, like the towel Top and Bottom Tabs, lengthen the stitches. Raise the presser foot, position the beginning of the seam under the needle and lower the needle.

Fold a scrap of fabric the same thickness as the seam and place the folded scrap behind the seam beginning. Lower the presser foot and begin stitching, holding out the thread tails.

13. Insert and pin the towel unit into the pressed opening of the Top Tab. Cover the towel seams with the Top Tab opening edges with hook-and-loop–tape side facing the Bottom Tab, referring to Figure 7. Hand-stitch Top Tab to towel top using a slip stitch to complete. ■

Figure 7

Gathering Edges

• Set stitch length at the longest length available on your machine. Thread machine with contrasting-color thread in needle and bobbin.

• Referring to Figure A, sew two rows of gathering stitches at ½ inch and ¼ inch from fabric edge to be gathered, leaving long thread tails at both ends. Start and stop gathering stitches at least the width of the seam allowance from the edges.

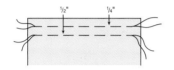 

Figure A   **Figure B**

• Place a pin at the fabric right-hand edge. Wrap the gathering thread tails around the pin (Figure B).

• Gather the fabric by pulling on the bobbin threads on left-hand side. As the fabric gathers, slide it along the top threads toward the pin (Figure C).

Figure C

• Continue gathering the fabric until it is the required length. Insert a second pin at the seam allowance on the left-hand fabric edge and wrap the threads around this pin to secure.

• Distribute the gathers evenly between the pins. Tie the top and bobbin threads into knots and remove the pins; trim thread tails.

• When construction is completed, remove gathering threads.

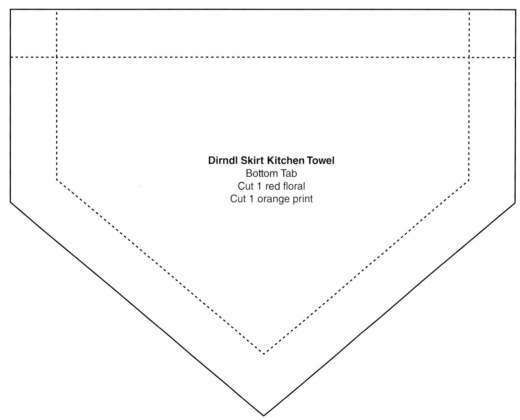

Dirndl Skirt Kitchen Towel
Bottom Tab
Cut 1 red floral
Cut 1 orange print

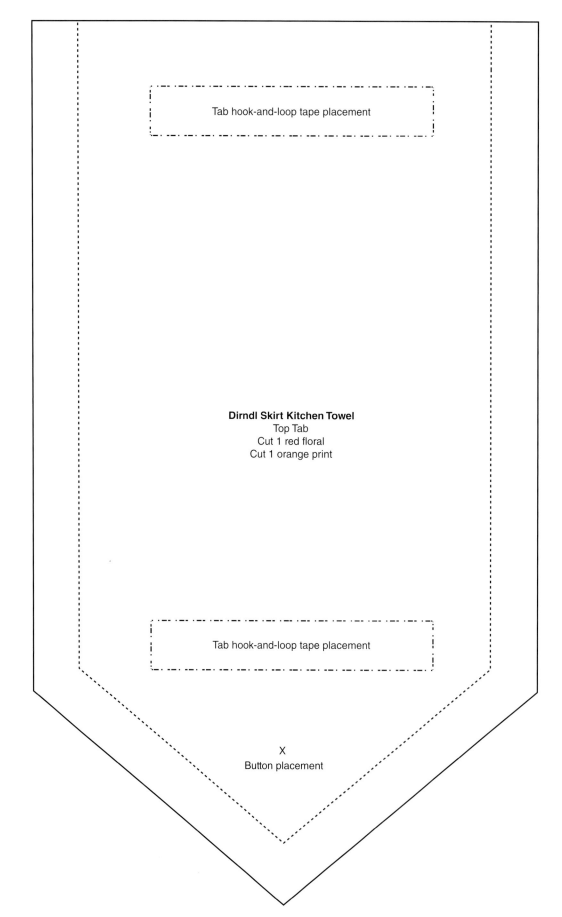

Tab hook-and-loop tape placement

Dirndl Skirt Kitchen Towel
Top Tab
Cut 1 red floral
Cut 1 orange print

Tab hook-and-loop tape placement

X
Button placement

To Market, to Market Produce Bag

Flowery cotton plus gauzy mesh equals the fresh new face of the produce bag. Forego plastic grocery bags and use this handy version so that at the supermarket or the farmer's market you can think globally and act fashionably.

Finished Size
12 x 16 inches

Materials
- ⅛ yard red print
- ¼ yard each green floral and orange print
- ⅓ yard polyester netting
- Coordinating thread
- 1 yard braided cord
- ¼-inch-wide basting tape
- 1 spring cord lock
- Seam sealant
- Basic sewing supplies and equipment

General Tip

Use this bag in a variety of ways. It would make a great lingerie or sweater laundry bag at this size, or maybe a toy bag for trips to Grandma's house. At the beach it could be used to corral small beach toys or wet swimsuits and towels. Extra clothes for messy toddlers could be stored and then replaced with the soiled items when needed.

Cutting

From red print:
- Cut 1 (3-inch x fabric width) strip.
    Subcut 1 (3 x 25-inch) strip for bag insert.

From green floral:
- Cut 1 (5-inch x fabric width) strip.
    Subcut 1 (5 x 25-inch) strip for bag top.

From orange print:
- Cut 1 (5-inch x fabric width) strip.
    Subcut 1 (5 x 25-inch) strip for bag bottom.

From polyester netting:
- Cut 1 (10-inch x fabric width) strip.
    Subcut 1 (10 x 25-inch) rectangle.

Sewing Techniques*
Machine stitching:
  Straight stitching
  Topstitching
  French seams
  Edgestitching
Refer to The Basics of Sewing on page 3.

Assembly

Use a ½-inch seam allowance and stitch right sides together unless otherwise indicated. Note that the first step of a French seam uses a ¼" seam allowance.

1. Using French seams and referring to Figure 1, stitch bag top to insert; stitch netting to insert and then stitch bag bottom to netting. Press seams toward insert and bottom, and edgestitch seam allowances in place referring to the red stitching lines in Figure 1.

Figure 1

Braided Cord Tips

• *Washable braided cord is available in cotton, polyester and nylon. It can be found in the home decor and trim sections of your fabric store.*

Look for braided cord, macramé braid, parachute cord, braided Polycord or rattail. You can also find nylon braided cord sold as nylon rope.

• *Use braided cord in sizes from ⅛ inch diameter to 1 inch diameter for bag handles depending on the size of the bag.*

• *When cutting braided cord, wrap tape around cord where it will be cut to keep cord from fraying after cutting.*

• *Tie knots in the ends of cotton cord after trimming taped ends.*

• *Carefully heat the ends of polyester and nylon cord with a lighter to melt the ends after trimming taped ends.*

• *Spring cord locks are perfect for cord handles. They allow you to secure the bag after closing it by sliding the fabric together on the cord and then sliding the lock along the cord, Look for different styles, including clips, and shapes, round and square.*

2. Stitch sides of bag together using a French seam stopping seam 2¼ inches from top of bag (Figure 2).

Figure 2

3. To create casing for cord handle, clip fabric to seam at top of side seam referring to blue dot on Figure 2. *Note: To keep fabric from fraying, place a dot of seam sealant at the clip.*

4. Fold edges at top of seam ¼ inch to wrong side; press. Repeat, folding ¼ inch to wrong side again; press and pin in place. Edgestitch along first fold referring to Figure 3. *Note: If desired, use basting tape to hold hem in place.*

Figure 3

5. Apply basting tape to right side of top edge of bag; fold top edge ¼ inch to wrong side (Figure 4). Fold again 1 inch to wrong side and press. Edgestitch along first fold, referring again to Figure 4.

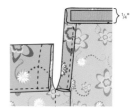

Figure 4

6. Attach safety pin to one end of cord and thread through casing.

7. Insert both ends of cord through spring cord lock. Tie knots in both ends of cord. ■

Customizing Bag Size

Customize the size of this bag for large laundry bags or shopping bags.

To enlarge the bag for a laundry bag:

• *Cut the bag top, insert and bottom the same widths indicated in the cutting instructions by the desired width x 2 plus 1 inch.*

• *Subtract 7¾ inches from the desired length. Cut the netting section this measurement plus 1 inch by the determined width.*

• *Cut pieces on the lengthwise grain of the fabric for larger bags if they are longer than the standard fabric width of 44/45 inches. Figure yardages needed by the determined width of the pieces.*

For example, for a 30 x 40-inch laundry bag:

• *Cut 1 each 5 x 61-inch bag top strip, 3 x 61-inch bag insert strip and 5 x 61-inch bag bottom strip from desired fabrics.*

• *Cut a 33¼ x 61-inch netting section.*

Note: You would need 1¾ yards of each fabric and netting to make a multicolored bag like the sample. For larger bags, it is more cost effective to use one or two fabrics for these pieces, or be creative and cut shorter strips across the fabric width or from scraps and then stitch them together to achieve the length needed.

Soft Spot Drying Mat

Kiss your kitchen storage problems goodbye! A colorful cushion provides the perfect spot to air-dry your dishes. When it's dry, fold it in half and slip it inside a drawer. Try doing that with a bulky rubber mat!

Finished Size
18 x 18 inches

Materials
- Fat quarter green print (optional)
- Fat quarter or ¼ yard each red floral and red print
- ⅝ yard nonskid fabric
- ⅝ yard foam stabilizer
- Coordinating thread
- ¼-inch-wide basting tape (optional)
- ½-inch-wide coordinating double-fold packaged bias tape (optional)
- Basic sewing supplies and equipment

Bias Tape Options
If you want bias binding that exactly matches your project, or you want it made from a subtle or a splashy print, try making your own. Refer to page 10 in the Basics of Sewing for instructions.

Cutting

From optional green print:
- If not purchasing bias tape, refer to Making Bias or Straight-Grain Seam Binding in The Basics of Sewing on page 10 to make at least 90 inches of bias tape.

From red floral:
- Cut 1 (8 x 18-inch) rectangle for center panel.

From red print:
- Cut 2 (6 x 18-inch) rectangles for sides.

From nonskid fabric:
- Cut 1 (18-inch) square.

From foam stabilizer:
- Cut 1 (18-inch) square.

Sewing Techniques*
Machine stitching:
  Straight stitching
  Topstitching
  Edgestitching
  Basting
Hand stitching:
  Basting
Refer to The Basics of Sewing on page 3.

Assembly

Use a ¼-inch seam allowance and stitch right sides together unless otherwise indicated.

1. Stitch a side rectangle on both long sides of the center panel to make mat top. Press seams toward sides. Topstitch ¼-inch from seam.

2. Layer and pin together: nonskid fabric, right side down; foam stabilizer; and mat top, right side up (Figure 1). Trim layers to match mat top if necessary. Baste layers together to assemble mat.

Figure 1

3. Align Corner Trimming Template (on page 42) with straight sides of mat and trim corners (Figure 2). Repeat for all four corners.

Figure 2

4. Cut 7 inches of bias tape. Edgestitch along both long edges; fold length in half to form a hanging loop. At center of one side of mat, match raw edges and baste in place using ⅛-inch seam allowance (Figure 3).

Figure 3

5. Open remaining bias tape and fold in short end ¼ inch to wrong side. Pin to nonskid side of mat matching raw edges (Figure 4a). Stitch along first fold referring again to Figure 4a and overlapping beginning end approximately 1 inch; trim off excess length.

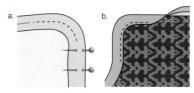

Figure 4

6. Turn bias tape to fabric side of mat and pin folded edge in place to cover seam. Topstitch the bias tape in place (Figure 4b). *Note: If you are having trouble pinning through the thickness of the layers, hold the bias tape in place with basting tape.* ▪

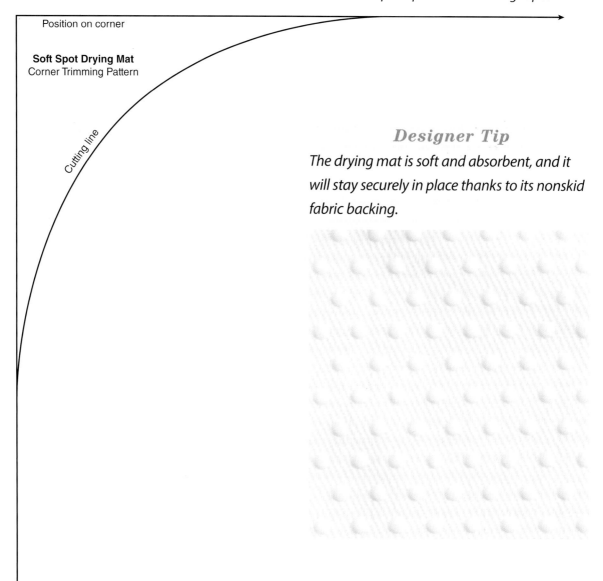

Position on corner

Soft Spot Drying Mat
Corner Trimming Pattern

Cutting line

Designer Tip

The drying mat is soft and absorbent, and it will stay securely in place thanks to its nonskid fabric backing.

Baker's Dozen Tote Bag

Design and dash with a carryall bag that is totally perfect! You will love it for its sturdy base and pleated sides, not to mention its interior divider, extra pockets and handy key holder. Stuff it with your favorite things and this tote will be totally you.

Finished Size
17 x 17 x 4 inches excluding handles

Materials
- 44/45-inch-wide 100 percent cotton fabric:
    - ¼ yard each red floral
    - ⅜ yard green print
    - ⅝ yard each cream print and orange print
    - ¾ yard red print
- Coordinating thread
- ⅛ yard heavy-weight fusible interfacing
- 1 yard ⅜-inch-wide elastic
- 1 (2-inch) carabiner hook
- 4 x 17-inch piece plastic canvas for stabilizer
- ¼-inch-wide basting tape (optional)
- Basic sewing supplies and equipment

Cutting

From red floral:
- Cut 1 (5-inch x fabric width) strip.
    Subcut 2 (5 x 22-inch) top band strips.
- Cut 1 (2¼-inch x fabric width) strip.
    Subcut 2 (2¼ x 22-inch) bag handles.

From green print:
- Cut 1 (2¼-inch x fabric width) strip.
    Subcut 2 (2¼ x 22-inch) bag handles.
- Cut 1 (9-inch x fabric width) strip.
    Subcut 1 (9 x 18½-inch) rectangle for
        bottom stabilizer cover.
    From remainder of strip, subcut
        1 (2 x 18-inch) strip for key fob.

From cream print:
- Cut 1 (18-inch x fabric width) strip.
    Subcut 1 (18 x 22-inch) inside divider.

From orange print:
- Cut 1 (18-inch x fabric width) strip.
    Subcut 1 (18 x 22-inch) bag front.

From red print:
- Cut 1 (18-inch x fabric width) rectangle.
    Subcut 1 (18 x 22-inch) bag back and
        1 (12 x 22-inch) front pocket.

From heavy-weight interfacing:
- Cut 2 (2 x 21-inch) strips.

Sewing Techniques*
Machine stitching:
  Straight stitching
  Topstitching
  Edgestitching
  French seams
Hand stitching:
  Basting
  Ladder stitch
*Refer to Sewing Techniques in The Basics of Sewing on page 3.

Assembly

Use a ½-inch seam allowance and stitch right sides together unless otherwise indicated. Note that the first step of a French seam uses a ¼" seam allowance.

1. Stitch top band to each of the front and back pieces using French seams. Press the seams away from the top bands and topstitch ¼ inch from seam.

2. Position heavy-weight fusible interfacing strips on wrong side of top bands against the seam referring to Figure 1; press.

Figure 1

3. Measuring on long sides, mark a line down the center of the front pocket on the right side.

4. Press front pocket top and bottom long edges to wrong side ¼ inch. Turn top edge 2 inches to wrong side and bottom edge ¼ inch to wrong side; press (Figure 2).

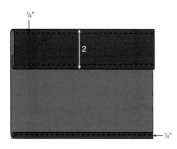

Figure 2

5. Edgestitch along second folds on top and bottom; topstitch ¼ inch from top folded edge referring again to Figure 2.

6. Position and pin front pocket, right side up, 2 inches up from right side of front bottom, matching side raw edges (Figure 3). Edgestitch pocket bottom edge.

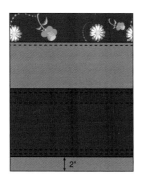

Figure 3

7. Topstitch along marked pocket centerline referring to Figure 3 and backstitching at top of centerline to reinforce pocket.

8. To make inside divider, fold divider in half right sides together lengthwise to make an 18 x 11-inch rectangle and stitch. Press seam open. Turn right side out and position seam at center back; press flat.

9. Topstitch ½ inch from top and bottom folds to create elastic casing referring to Figure 4.

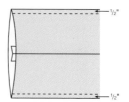

Figure 4

10. Cut two 15-inch pieces of elastic. Attach a safety pin to one end of an elastic piece and thread through casing. Pin beginning and end of elastic to casing openings to secure; baste elastic in place at side seams. Repeat for second casing. Set aside.

11. To make key fob, fold 2 x 18-inch strip in half right sides together lengthwise and stitch long raw edges together.

12. Turn right side out and press flat. Edgestitch both long edges.

13. Thread remaining 6 inches of elastic through tube; pin both ends of elastic and baste to secure.

14. Turn one end of tube over ¼ inch and again 1 inch. Edgestitch along first fold to create a loop.

15. Position and pin key fob raw end to side of wrong side of bag front just below the top band seam. Position and pin inside divider to bag front wrong side 2½ inches up from bottom edge. Baste key fob and divider along sides to hold in place referring to Figure 5.

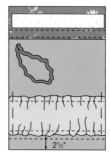

Figure 5

16. Fold bag front and back top band edges ¼ inch to wrong side and press. Fold again over interfacing with band top folded edge even with band bottom seam; edgestitch along band top folded edge (Figure 6).

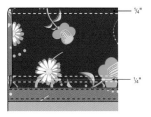

Figure 6

17. Topstitch ¼ inch from top fold and ¼ inch from edgestitching referring again to Figure 6.

18. Stitch bag side seams matching band seams and using French seams.

19. Measure and mark a line 2 inches from side seams on both front and back top bands (Figure 7).

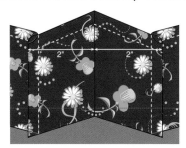

Figure 7

20. Fold bands wrong sides together along marked lines; press and topstitch ½ inch from fold the length of band referring again to Figure 7. Repeat to make four corners.

21. Stitch a red floral and a green print handle pieces together on both long sides. Repeat to make two handles. Turn right side out and press flat.

22. Topstitch ¼ inch from long sides of handles. Turn green print side 1½ inches to red floral side on both ends and press (Figure 8). Repeat with second handle.

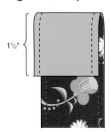

Figure 8

23. Position and pin handles to top band 3 inches from topstitched band folded edge and slightly below band bottom edge referring to Figure 9.

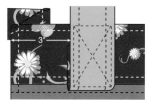

Figure 9

24. Topstitch in place, edgestitching a box on handle end and then stitching diagonally through box referring to red stitching lines in Figure 9. Repeat for all handle ends.

25. Turn bag wrong side out and stitch bottom seam of bag. Finish seam with zigzag stitches. Press to one side.

26. To box bottom of bag, match side seam to bottom seam forming a triangle at corner (Figure 10). Stitch across corner triangle 2 inches from point referring again to Figure 10. Trim seam allowance to ¼ inch and finish seam edge with zigzag stitches. Repeat on opposite corner.

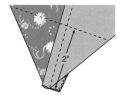

Figure 10

27. Fold bottom stabilizer cover in half lengthwise; stitch one short end and long raw edge together (Figure 11). Turn right side out and insert plastic canvas stabilizer.

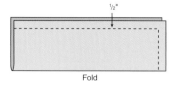

Fold

Figure 11

28. Fold open end to inside and hand-stitch closed using a ladder stitch. Insert into bottom of bag.

29. Attach carabiner hook for key fob. ■

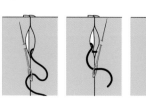

Ladder Stitch

Learn Easy Sewing Skills

Photo Index

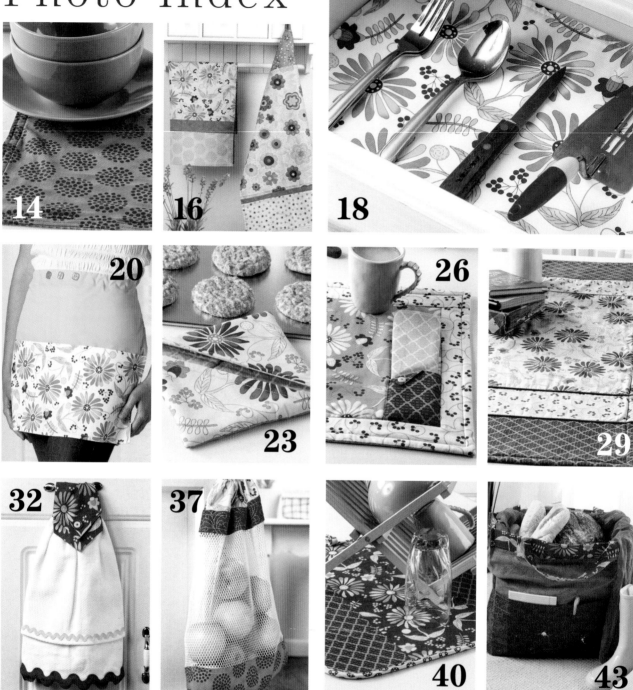

14

16

18

20

23

26

29

32

37

40

43

Annie's ®

RETAIL STORES: If you would like to carry this pattern book or any other Annie's publications, visit AnniesWSL.com.

Every effort has been made to ensure that the instructions in this pattern book are complete and accurate. We cannot, however, take responsibility for human error, typographical mistakes or variations in individual work. Please visit AnniesCustomerCare.com to check for pattern updates.

ISBN: 978-1-57367-576-5

1 2 3 4 5 6 7 8 9